For Dorothy

who has been helping us
keep the truck among the trees

with thanks and admiration

William

Nov 20 1991

Books by W. S. Merwin

The Rain in the Trees

Hawaii 90% Species
= unique to H.

50% on endangered
List.

WROP: 25,000 Acres

nr Puna

<u>Geothermal Corps:</u>

Ormat
True Venture

<u>man's unique
Capacity</u> - see beyond
ourselves to other
selves + other creatures.

The Rain in the Trees

POEMS BY W. S. Merwin

New York ALFRED A. KNOPF *1991*

THIS IS A BORZOI BOOK
PUBLISHED BY ALFRED A. KNOPF, INC.

SOME OF THESE POEMS WERE ORIGINALLY PUBLISHED IN THE FOLLOWING PERIODICALS:

AMERICAN POETRY REVIEW: SIGHT, COMING TO THE MORNING, KNOCK, COMING TO HEAR, TO THE INSECTS, THE BIOLOGY OF ART, FOR THE DEPARTURE OF A STEPSON, TRACING THE LETTERS, THE ARCHAIC MAKER

ANTAEUS: LATE SPRING, WEST WALL

THE ATLANTIC MONTHLY: CHORD

CALIBAN: LEARNING, THE STRANGERS FROM THE HORIZON, THE LOST ORIGINALS

FIELD: HEARING THE NAMES OF THE VALLEYS, THE DUCK, MEMORY

GRAND STREET: BEFORE US, TOUCHING THE TREE, SHADOW PASSING, NOTES FROM A JOURNEY, PASTURES, THE HORIZONS OF ROOMS

IOWA REVIEW: SKY IN SEPTEMBER. NATIVE TREES, MEMENTOS, NIGHT ABOVE THE AVENUE, AT THE SAME TIME, WAYS, NOTE IN A GUIDEBOOK

MEMPHIS STATE REVIEW: ANNIVERSARY ON THE ISLAND

THE NATION: WAKING TO THE RAIN, UTTERANCE, PAPER, THANKS, PLACE

THE NEW YORKER: THE FIRST YEAR, SUMMER '82, THE SOUND OF THE LIGHT, NOW RENTING, GLASSES, HISTORY, AFTER SCHOOL, THE SALT POND, LIBERTY, JOURNEY, AIRPORT, KANALOA, THE ROSE BEETLE, THE SUPERSTITION

THE PARIS REVIEW: THE SOLSTICE, BEING EARLY, CONQUEROR

OHIO REVIEW: TERM

PARTISAN REVIEW: EMPTY WATER, THE INEVITABLE LIGHTNESS, SNOW

POETRY: AFTER THE ALPHABETS, A LAST LOOK, THE OVERPASS

THE YALE REVIEW: NATIVE, LOSING A LANGUAGE

Library of Congress Cataloging-in-Publication Data

Merwin, W. S. (William Stanley), [date]
　　The rain in the trees.

　　　I. Title.
PS3563.E75R35　1988　　811.'54　　　87–46081
ISBN 0–394–57039–1
ISBN 0–394–75858–7 (pbk.)

Manufactured in the United States of America
Published April 1, 1988
Reprinted Once
Third Printing, March 1991

For Paula

Contents

Handwritten annotations:

after reading, (1992) Look for Poem "The Last One" in another volume - (collected Poems 'Lice) p 118 — Look for Book (prose on France.) Look for other poetry volumes, New one in 1992 (Travels)

also on CBS 5/95

T. Gross '88 interview replayed 5/95

parents

last line

KG

KB

Terry Gross interview '88 replayed 5/9 5

Contents

The Rain in the Trees

LATE SPRING

Coming into the high room again after years
after oceans and shadows of hills and the sounds of lies
after losses and feet on stairs

after looking and mistakes and forgetting
turning there thinking to find
no one except those I knew
finally I saw you
sitting in white
already waiting

you of whom I had heard
with my own ears since the beginning
for whom more than once
I had opened the door
believing you were not far

WEST WALL

In the unmade light I can see the world
as the leaves brighten I see the air
the shadows melt and the apricots appear
now that the branches vanish I see the apricots
from a thousand trees ripening in the air
they are ripening in the sun along the west wall
apricots beyond number are ripening in the daylight

Whatever was there
I never saw those apricots swaying in the light
I might have stood in orchards forever
without beholding the day in the apricots
or knowing the ripeness of the lucid air
or touching the apricots in your skin
or tasting in your mouth the sun in the apricots

THE FIRST YEAR

When the words had all been used
for other things
we saw the first day begin

out of the calling water
and the black branches
leaves no bigger than your fingertips
were unfolding on the tree of heaven
against the old stained wall
their green sunlight
that had never shone before

waking together we were the first
to see them
and we knew them then

all the languages were foreign and the first
year rose

NATIVE TREES

Neither my father nor my mother knew
the names of the trees
where I was born
what is that
I asked and my
father and mother did not
hear they did not look where I pointed
surfaces of furniture held
the attention of their fingers
and across the room they could watch
walls they had forgotten
where there were no questions
no voices and no shade

Were there trees
where they were children
where I had not been
I asked
were there trees in those places
where my father and my mother were born
and in that time did
my father and my mother see them
and when they said yes it meant
they did not remember
What were they I asked what were they
but both my father and my mother
said they never knew

TOUCHING THE TREE

Faces are bending over me asking why

they do not live here they do not know anything
there is a black river beyond the buildings
watching everything from one side
it is moving while I touch the tree

the black river says no my father says no
my mother says no in the streets they say nothing
they walk past one at a time in hats
with their heads down
it is wrong to answer them through the green fence
the street cars go by singing to themselves *I am iron*
the broom seller goes past in the sound of grass
by the tree touching the tree I hear the tree
I walk with the tree
we talk without anything

come late echoes of ferries chains whistles
tires on the avenue wires humming among windows
words flying out of rooms
the stones of the wall are painted white to be better
but at the foot of the tree in the fluttering light
I have dug a cave for a lion
a lion cave so that the cave will be there
among the roots waiting
when the lion comes to the tree

NIGHT ABOVE THE AVENUE

The whole time that I have lived here
at every moment somebody
has been at the point of birth
behind a window across the street
and somebody behind a window
across the street
has been at the point of death
they have lain there in pain and in hope
on and on
and away from the windows the dark interiors
of their bodies have been opened to lights
and they have waited bleeding and have been frightened
and happy
unseen by each other we have been transformed
and the traffic has flowed away
from between them and me
in four directions
as the lights have changed
day and night
and I have sat up late
at the kitchen window
knowing the news
watching the paired red lights
recede from under the windows down the avenue
toward the tunnel under the river
and the white lights from the park rushing toward us
through the sirens and the music
and I have wakened in a wind of messages

NOW RENTING

Nobody remembers
the original site
of course
what was there to remember

somebody
nobody remembers
wanted a little building
nobody knows why

on the original site
and cleared it
no doubt
had to

later somebody
wanted a little
more space
and set up a scaffold

around the first building
and built the walls higher
and then tore down
the scaffold

then in time somebody
put up more scaffolding
and tore down
the whole building

and dug a hole
in the original site
and put up a bigger
building and tore

down the scaffolding
to the accompaniment
of music announcing
a golden age

but somebody with vision
soon put more scaffolding
on top of the building
and raised the whole structure

even higher than before
and tore down the scaffolding
but a while after that
somebody put up more scaffolding

clear above the top of the building
and tore down the building inside it
and went on adding scaffolding
with glass pictures on it

all the way up
of a glass building
never built
on that site

with nobody
inside it
at all the windows
to see the motionless clouds

GLASSES

There is no eye to catch

They come in uniforms
they cross bridges built on cement arches
they dip their lights
they wave

they have just read a book
they have never read a book
they have just turned from the TV
they have just turned from the table
or bed

it is morning and they pour
one by one out of the door
they are real glass and thin
and the wind is blowing
the sky is racing
they come to drink from the steel fountain
they come to walk on the carpet
they come past the doors
of frosted glass

they turn in the window at the end of the hall
in amber light
ninety floors from the ground
walking on empty evening
they pay the electric bills
they owe money
all the stars turn in vast courses around them
unnoticed
they vote

they buy their tickets
they applaud
they go into the elevator
thinking of money
with the quiet gleam of money

Glasses

they bear arms
they go on wheels they are without color
they come in clothes out of closets
they fly above the earth reading papers
the bulldozers make way for them
they glitter under imported leaves

SHADOW PASSING

Suddenly in bright sunlight small clouds
and on a map I remember
we were growing toward us
like lights in the distance

it was a country of mines
and faces like sawed bones
sitting outside their black doorways
staring into tunnels in the daylight

the rivers and the standing
water were full
of the dreams of presidents
of coal companies

and from the churches
on the flayed slopes
rose hymns of resurrection
then the sunlight came back

HISTORY

Only I never came back

the gates stand open
where I left the barnyard in the evening
as the owl was bringing the mouse home
in the gold sky
at the milking hour
and I turned to the amber hill and followed
along the gray fallen wall
by the small mossed oaks and the bushes of rusting
arches bearing the ripe
blackberries into the long shadow
and climbed the ancient road
through the last songs of the blackbirds

passing the last live farms
their stones running with dark liquid
and the ruined farms their windows without frames
facing away
looking out across the pastures of dead shepherds
whom nobody ever knew
grown high with the dry flowers of late summer
their empty doorways gazing
toward the arms of the last oaks
and at night their broken chimneys watching
the cold of the meteors

the beams had fallen together
to rest in brown herds around the fireplaces
and in the shade of black trees the houses were full
of their own fragrance at last
mushrooms and owls
and the song of the cicadas

there was a note on a page
made at the time
and the book was closed
and taken on a journey
into a country where no one
knew the language

no one could read
even the address
inside the cover
and there the book was
of course lost

it was a book full of words to remember
this is how we manage without them
this is how they manage
without us

I was not going to be long

NOTES FROM A JOURNEY

Ringed by shadowy balconies
paint peeling from the old beams
the echoing squares paved in marble
a thousand years ago
climb the slope like shallow terraces
tall grass twitching above the cracks
and the thin cats watching the light

*

All the way down the peninsula
the walls of the crumbling farms are the colors
of evening
we who are going wait in stone courtyards
until everything is in order
loops of leather hang in the shadows
by a ruined doorway next to me
as I sit on the bench and stroke the lioness
and the big horses sigh by the gate

*

Last night the beautiful
woman in whose house I stayed
told of finding a prostitute
half dead of exhaustion in the street
unable to speak
and bringing her home and putting her
into the woman's own bed
she said
and in the night looking and seeing a light
coming from the bed and from the figure there
a gold light that filled the room with blessing
and no one was there in the morning
what am I to make of such a story
having been given the same bed

*

No horses now for days
cracked whitewash in the old streets of the south
on an upper story the dark ceiling of a kitchen
the women preparing a meal their hands full of dough

laughing
some of them very old
they call me to come up
and sit at the long table
and eat
the daughters talk to me as though they knew me

*

Near the harbor
as the afternoon was turning blue
this cafe on a side street
everything standing open no one to be seen
the facade of the building like a huge mosque
blank
white
an arched doorway with curtains drawn back
the curtains too carved in gray stone
inside it was cool and shady
a man and a woman stood under a tree
at the foot of the marble stairs in the courtyard
and asked me whether I wanted to sleep there
and as I left in the morning
I saw that the wall at the end of the courtyard
was full of sky from which the stones had fallen

*

I stepped from the end of a street
into a square so wide that the buildings around it
appeared to be melting like mirages on the horizon
and I thought it had happened before
gray marble and twilight and sun setting in mist
I was on my way to meet friends
with whom I was to travel the next day
and of course I was late
and forgot to find out the name of the street

*

I turn the corners in the small steep seaport
no bigger than a village
with the feeling that I once knew it
and that it has changed in the interval

like someone who remembers me as a child
the old town hall has been abandoned
and for several years the lower floor has been flooded
I was sure I remembered the old
grandfather clock standing there
with its feet in water and its shoulders
fallen against the arch of the far window
its pendulum rod loose in the air
and for a moment I wanted to rescue it
and take it with me

*

Walking along the edge of the sea cliffs
with the light on the yellow crags below me
country of quarries
wagons loaded with stones and the horses
struggling and slipping on the cart tracks
for no reason that they know
and I see that each of the stones is numbered

*

Breakfast with a wagon driver's
family in the mountains
it is a day commemorating
a liberation
we have peaches and little hot loaves
under the trees by the kitchen
which has a roof but no walls
most of the stones he tells me
are quarried and carted illegally
so that too has to be paid for

*

I have been staying
in the empty fisherman's house
facing out to sea
the whole village is abandoned now
the doorways echoing the dark patios
there is a hall behind the stairwell
and from the end of the hall too
the sea shines

a lifeboat is half buried in the rocks
above the water line
there I met a heavy woman in black
walking along the shore
a caretaker she said
who knew everybody

*

A room in back of a shop
in the mountains
there is dancing after dark
and they get drunk and keep giving
presents to the stranger
who happens to be me
clothes a little worn
which I have to try on and keep
and a big knife on a belt
then a bitter argument
begins and builds
I think I had better leave
and I walk out into the rain and the night
not knowing how to thank them

*

At the end of a long bay
in sloping country blonde with straw
before autumn
how they love to eat and they all cook
at table they tell of the time when they were all
taken away
and the children know the story
and listen

*

At night I dreamed that I was far away
and that I lived there
finally I took the boat
from the foot of the mountain
and thought I knew where I was going
and that it was still there

PASTURES

Some who are still alive
grew up in them
and when they could barely walk
ran with the sheep
and came to the gate

one time boys watching sheep
in the upland pastures
on the day of the fair
saw a man they knew
come and wait

for a woman they knew
and kill her with a rock
and they hid
under a flowering
honeysuckle

I was taught the word
pasture as though
it came from the Bible
but I knew it named something
with a real sky

one day my mother
and the woman we were visiting
wanted to talk about things
they did not want me to hear

so I walked out past the pig pen
under the apple trees
and the first pigs I had seen
alive
crowded to the corner
to look at me

I passed the barn
where bands of light
reached between the boards
to touch the back of sheep

standing and doing
nothing in the shadow

and went up the green track
to the top of the ridge
and saw the open
pasture sloping
away to the woods
it was another sky
a day of its own
it was the night pasture

as children
we ran among
mounds of rusting ferns
in the long sunset
of an endless summer
our thin voices
spinning across the still pasture
calling each other

and we hid
in the chill twilight
face down hearing our breaths
our own breaths
full of the horizon
and the smell of the dew
on the cold ferns

even then
in the spring
there were those on earth
who drove flocks
from winter pastures
near the sea
up into the green slopes
enclosed by woods
in the mountains

Pastures

they went all together
it took ten days
before they came
to the summer pastures
they said were theirs
full of tall
young grass
many
now do not know
any such thing

AFTER SCHOOL

For a long time I wanted
to get out of that school
where I had been sent
for the best

I thought of climbing
down the vine
outside the window
at night

after the watchman
had turned the corner
to the boiler room
in the sweet autumn dark

I wanted to slip
through the still dining hall
and down the cellar stairs
in the girls' wing

where I had set the waltzing
in the first book
of *War and Peace*
I would pass unseen in that crowd

into the cellar
and the secret door to the steam pipes
and under the street
to the swimming pool

I would have persuaded
a girl I liked
to meet me there
and we would swim whispering

because of the echoes
while the light from the street
shone through the frosted windows
like the light of the moon

all down the hot room
where the sound of the water
made the heart beat loud
to think of it

but I never
got away then
and when I think now
of following that tunnel

there is a black wolf
tied there waiting
a thin bitch
who snaps at my right hand

but I untie her
and we find our way
out of there as one
and down the street

hungry
nobody in sight at that hour
everything closed
behind us

EMPTY WATER

I miss the toad
who came all summer
to the limestone
water basin
under the Christmasberry tree
imported in 1912
from Brazil for decoration
then a weed on a mule track
on a losing
pineapple plantation
now an old tree in a line
of old trees
the toad came at night
first and sat in the water
all night and all day
then sometimes at night
left for an outing
but was back in the morning
under the branches among
the ferns the green sword leaf
of the lily
sitting in the water
all the dry months
gazing at the sky
through those eyes
fashioned of the most
precious of metals
come back
believer in shade
believer in silence and elegance
believer in ferns
believer in patience
believer in the rain

RAIN AT NIGHT

This is what I have heard

at last the wind in December
lashing the old trees with rain
unseen rain racing along the tiles
under the moon
wind rising and falling
wind with many clouds
trees in the night wind

after an age of leaves and feathers
someone dead
thought of this mountain as money
and cut the trees
that were here in the wind
in the rain at night
it is hard to say it
but they cut the sacred 'ohias then
the sacred koas then
the sandalwood and the halas
holding aloft their green fires
and somebody dead turned cattle loose
among the stumps until killing time

but the trees have risen one more time
and the night wind makes them sound
like the sea that is yet unknown
the black clouds race over the moon
the rain is falling on the last place

WAKING TO THE RAIN

The night of my birthday
I woke from a dream
of harmony
suddenly hearing
an old man not my father
I said but it was
my father gasping
my name as he fell
on the stone steps outside
just under the window
in the rain
I do not know
how many times
he may have called
before I woke
I was lying
in my parents' room
in the empty house
both of them dead
that year
and the rain was falling
all around me
the only sound

THE SALT POND

Mid September   my dead father's birthday
again by the low shore I watch the gulls fly inland
white gulls riding a knowledge older than they are

by now you are eighty eight and need nothing old friend
twelve years in the white sky out of the wind

once more at the end of summer the first map of the coast
looks out from the wall
a shadow imperceptibly darkening
the names dissolve across it
white clouds race over the marshes

the gulls have gone with their age
I know the wind

SUMMER '82

When it was already autumn
we heard of the terrible weather
we had lived through
heat in the city and rain
in the filthy streets

but to us it looked new
night and day
in the washed crowds I could see
after so many lives you
and through the blurred sirens and the commercials
and the hissing of buses on Fifth
I could hear at last what I
had listened for
we woke in the night holding
each other
trying to believe we were there
in that summer among those
same towers

in first light we both remembered
one house deep among leaves
the steps the long porch the breeze at the door
the rooms one by one and the windows
the hours and what they looked out on
nothing had given up

we were swallowed into the subway in the morning
together we sifted
along the sidewalks in the glare
we saw friends again
each time as though
returning after a war
and laughed and embraced them
on a corner in the ringing downpour

and in the evening we alone
took the streetcar to the rain forest
followed the green ridge in the dusk
got off to walk home through the ancient trees

BEFORE US

You were there all the time and I saw only
the days the air
the nights the moon changing
cars passing and faces at windows
the windows
the rain the leaves the years
words on pages telling of something else
wind in a mirror

everything begins so late after all
when the solitaires have already gone
and the doves of Tanna
when the Laughing Owls have
long been followed by question marks
and honeycreepers and the brown
bears of Atlas
the white wolf and the sea mink have not been seen
by anyone living

we wake so late after many dreams
it is clear
when the lake has vanished
the shepherds have left the shielings
grandparents have dissolved with their memories
dictionaries are full of graves
most of the rivers are lethal
we thought we were younger
through all those ages of knowing nothing
and there you are
at last after such fallings away and voyages
beside me in the dawning

we wake together and the world is here in its dew
you are here and the morning is whole
finally the light is young
because it is here it is not like anything
how could it have taken you so long to appear
bloom of air tenderness of leaves
where were you when the lies were voting
and the fingers believed faces on money

where were we when the smoke washed us
and the hours cracked as they rang
where was I when we passed each other
on the same streets
and travelled by the same panes to the same stations

now we have only the age that is left
to be together
the brief air the vanishing green
ordure in office tourists on the headland
the last hours of the sea
now we have only the words we remember
to say to each other
only the morning of your eyes and the day
of our faces to be together
only the time of our hands with its vexed
motor and the note
of the thrush on the guava branch in the shining rain
for the rest of our lives

THE SOUND OF THE LIGHT

I hear sheep running on the path of broken limestone
through brown curled leaves fallen early from walnut limbs
at the end of a summer how light the bony
flutter of their passage I can
hear their coughing their calling and wheezing even the warm
greased wool rubbing on the worn walls I hear them
passing passing in the hollow lane and there is still time

the shuffle of black shoes of women climbing
stone ledges to church keeps flowing up the dazzling hill
around the grassy rustle of voices
on the far side of a slatted shutter
and the small waves go on whispering on the shingle
in the heat of an hour without wind it is Sunday
none of the sentences begins or ends there is time

again the unbroken rumble of trucks and the hiss
of brakes roll upward out of the avenue
I forget what season they are exploding through
what year the drill on the sidewalk is smashing
it is the year in which you are sitting there as you are
in the morning speaking to me and I hear
you through the burning day and I touch you
to be sure and there is time there is still time

SKY IN SEPTEMBER

In spite of the months of knowing
and the years
autumn comes with astonishment
light held up in a glass
the terrible news in a haze
caught breath in the warm leaves

in spite of the gathered dust and the vast moon
the day comes with a color
its words cannot touch
so it is when I see you
after the years when the ailanthus leaves
drifted unnoticed
down the gray wall

they have disappeared and nothing is missing
after their rocking and clinging
they have vanished with the thieves and shufflers
and the words of the dealers
taking nothing
they have fallen like scales from the eyes
and at last we are here together
light of autumn
clear morning in the only time

ANNIVERSARY ON THE ISLAND

The long waves glide in through the afternoon
while we watch from the island
from the cool shadow under the trees where the long ridge
a fold in the skirt of the mountain
runs down to the end of the headland

day after day we wake to the island
the light rises through the drops on the leaves
and we remember like birds where we are
night after night we touch the dark island
that once we set out for

and lie still at last with the island in our arms
hearing the leaves and the breathing shore
there are no years any more
only the one mountain
and on all sides the sea that brought us

SIGHT

Once
a single cell
found that it was full of light
and for the first time there was seeing

when
I was a bird
I could see where the stars had turned
and I set out on my journey

high
in the head of a mountain goat
I could see across a valley
under the shining trees something moving

deep
in the green sea
I saw two sides of the water
and swam between them

I
look at you
in the first light of the morning
for as long as I can

THE SOLSTICE

They say the sun will come back
at midnight
after all
my one love

but we know how the minutes
fly out into
the dark trees
and vanish

like the great ohias and the honey creepers
and we know how the weeks
walk into the
shadows at midday

at the thought of the months I reach for your hand
it is not something
one is supposed
to say

we watch the bright birds in the morning
we hope for the quiet
daytime together
the year turns into air

but we are together in the whole night
with the sun still going away
and the year
coming back

COMING TO THE MORNING

You make me remember all of the elements
the sea remembering all of its waves

in each of the waves there was always a sky made of water
and an eye that looked once

there was the shape of one mountain
and a blood kinship with rain

and the air for touch and for the tongue
at the speed of light

in which the world is made
from a single star

and our ears
are formed of the sea as we listen

BEING EARLY

When you were born
I was a small child in a city
and even if somebody had brought me news of you
I would not have believed them

already I had seen an ape chained in the sun
with a bucket of water
I had heard bells calling from wooden towers
stone towers brick towers
I had seen blood coming through bandages
on a hand holding candy
and a shadow shining on green water
where tall birds were standing
and I knew the notes of street cars
and the smells of three rivers
and could have told you about all of them
if I had known you were there

TRAVELLING TOGETHER

If we are separated I will
try to wait for you
on your side of things

your side of the wall and the water
and of the light moving at its own speed
even on leaves that we have seen
I will wait on one side

while a side is there

THE INEVITABLE LIGHTNESS

The roads and everything on them fly up and dissolve
a net rises from the world
the cobweb in which it was dying
and the earth breathes naked with its new scars
and sky everywhere

THE CRUST

Sire it is true as far
as it goes
it was summer and a holiday
in the morning

and the traffic was piled on the roads
blocked at an intersection
with the radios playing
and I could see just ahead
that the earth had fallen away
from the road
underneath

I tried to get others to go back
and some began to go back
as the road opened under them

in my view it happened
that the earth fell from under
because the tree was cut
whose roots held it together
and with the tree
went all the lives in it
that slept in it ate in it
met in it believed in it
for whom it was all there was
the sun travelled to come back to it
it had evolved the only language
it remembered everything
but what do I know I am only a witness

the roots became cracks
and from the tree your chair was made
with the earth falling away from under it

MEMENTOS

Sunflowers are brought to me on the morning of your death
in the clear day hands you did not see
a face unknown to you and never expected
accompany the stems through the gate
repeating an unfamiliar
name under a few high clouds

beyond the flowers there is still the sea
beyond the writing the waves go on overflowing
here is a long envelope
from which a picture of a black lake emerges
far away between my fingers while the trees are flying

a friend with a passion for freedom
said a piece of a poem and got it wrong
and put it in a letter to me
it was a passage by someone
of whom she knew I thought little
and she sent it
to surprise and remind me but she
misquoted it and wrote *Even*
the newt the worm the germ the first spit
sing the day in full cry

and how does it go now

PRINT FALLEN OUT OF SOMEWHERE

It asks me to imagine a day with no colors
except brown

in a field with two children
in summer
the hour growing late
at the turn of a century
beside a pasture
full of brown cows
on whose backs a shadow
of the same color
floats
crouched over a camera

even from here I can see
it is a place where the children
do not live
and which they will not see again
with its unheard crickets
dry barn afternoon light
in which the boy in the white shirt
who will not live long
stands happily holding a horse
and the girl wearing
a tan hair ribbon
is frowning at the sun

it has come this far to show me
how they look straight at me
without seeing me

UTTERANCE

Sitting over words
very late I have heard a kind of whispered sighing
not far
like a night wind in pines or like the sea in the dark
the echo of everything that has ever
been spoken
still spinning its one syllable
between the earth and silence

PAPER

What an idea
that you can put it on a piece of paper
what is a piece of paper and how can you tell
put it on a piece of paper

at the beginning
there are the tall sub-polar mountains
above a peninsula
set in a plain of ice
under deep snow
from which the light comes
white no longer there
put it on that paper

the sound of the runners
in all that unpeopled day
at one with the wind and the breathing of the white dogs
and the wind wiping out the tracks at once
the white earth turning around and the sense of climbing
put it on that paper

everything is white so it can disappear
everything that is not white
is alone
the colors are all white
the night is white in a place not remembered
everything is the same color as the other planets
here in this place hard to see
on a piece of paper

THANKS

Listen
with the night falling we are saying thank you
we are stopping on the bridges to bow from the railings
we are running out of the glass rooms
with our mouths full of food to look at the sky
and say thank you
we are standing by the water thanking it
standing by the windows looking out
in our directions

back from a series of hospitals back from a mugging
after funerals we are saying thank you
after the news of the dead
whether or not we knew them we are saying thank you

over telephones we are saying thank you
in doorways and in the backs of cars and in elevators
remembering wars and the police at the door
and the beatings on stairs we are saying thank you
in the banks we are saying thank you
in the faces of the officials and the rich
and of all who will never change
we go on saying thank you thank you

with the animals dying around us
taking our feelings we are saying thank you
with the forests falling faster than the minutes
of our lives we are saying thank you
with the words going out like cells of a brain
with the cities growing over us
we are saying thank you faster and faster
with nobody listening we are saying thank you
thank you we are saying and waving
dark though it is

AT THE SAME TIME

So it seems there are only
our contemporaries
and we learn only from them listen only to them
talk only to them
after all there are no others

for the dead do not listen to us
out of the past
after everything they said
about us

and as for the future
what good would it do us
to be discovered
a hundred years on
with this sky gone from these valleys
and these valleys unknown

and what would the finders
think they had found
that was us
as they struggled to memorize
the old books of addresses

where we are talking and writing

COMING TO HEAR

He who insisted that he could not hear music
is floating over a dark sea
on which the lights

accompany him
wave upon wave
unseen and unbroken

there is a line of black trees
just over the horizon
on an island

which he will think familiar
now it is the sixth night
and he is hearing the colors

the sound of blue at night
that believes in nothing as always
is carrying him

TO THE INSECTS

Elders

we have been here so short a time
and we pretend that we have invented memory

we have forgotten what it is like to be you
who do not remember us

we remember imagining that what survived us
would be like us

and would remember the world as it appears to us
but it will be your eyes that will fill with light

we kill you again and again
and we turn into you

eating the forests
eating the earth and the water

and dying of them
departing from ourselves

leaving you the morning
in its antiquity

49

AFTER THE ALPHABETS

I am trying to decipher the language of insects
they are the tongues of the future
their vocabularies describe buildings as food
they can depict dark water and the veins of trees
they can convey what they do not know
and what is known at a distance
and what nobody knows
they have terms for making music with the legs
they can recount changing in a sleep like death
they can sing with wings
the speakers are their own meaning in a grammar without horizons
they are wholly articulate
they are never important they are everything

THE SUPERSTITION

The cars are disappearing
and we were told they were real
they were only what we thought of them
we were taught that they were beautiful
but we forgot them
we believed they were strong
but they were hauled away
we thought they would take us anywhere
but they had to stop
we thought they were fast and we have left them far behind
we believed they would save our lives
and we gave our lives for them
thinking they were worth it
we watched them pass with no beginning no end
glass on all sides
we dreamed of them and we woke
with the headlights flying through us

THE OVERPASS

You know how you
will be looking for somewhere
and come by surprise on a long cement bridge
sailing out over a wide
cement ditch carved deep into the hill
between whose banks the traffic is rushing
in both directions

in what is now the air above it
there was a pasture
beside dark woods
I saw it
and a swamp near the first trees
with a pump house hidden
in low green blackberry bushes
and mist coming off the upland marsh
first thing in the morning

and on the cold hill
a man and a boy
planting potatoes
with a mule keeping ahead of them
climbing the furrows
through the morning smelling of
wet grass
none of them seeing
the white bird flying over

SNOW

Comes the dust falling in the air
comes in the afternoon the sunbeam
comes through the sound of friends
comes the shadow through the door
comes the unturned page comes the name comes the footstep
comes to each wall the portrait
comes the white hair

comes with the flowers opening
comes as the hands touch and stay
comes with late fortune and late seed
comes with the whole of music
comes with the light on the mountains
comes at the hours of clouds
comes the white hair

comes the sudden widening of the river
comes as the birds disappear in the air
comes while we talk together
comes as we listen to each other
comes as we are lying together
comes while we sleep
comes the white hair

FOR THE DEPARTURE OF A STEPSON

You are going for a long time
and nobody knows what to expect

we are trying to learn
not to accompany gifts with advice

or to suppose that we can protect you
from being changed

by something that we do not know
but have always turned away from

even by the sea that we love
with its breaking

and the dissolving days
and the shadows on the wall

together we look at the young trees
we read the news we smell the morning

we cannot tell you what to take with you
in your light baggage

AIRPORT

None of the computers can say
how long it took to evolve a facility
devoted to absence in life

you walk out of the chute
and a person smiles at your ticket
and points you to your seat

is this the only way home
nobody asks
because nobody knows

the building is not inhabited it is not
home except to roaches
it is not loved it is serviced

it is not a place
but a container with signs
directing a process

there is neither youth in the air
nor earth under foot
there is a machine to announce

yet the corridors beat with anguish longing relief
news trash insurance dispensers
and many are glad to be here

thinking of being somewhere else
hurrying at great expense
across glass after glass

we travel far and fast
and as we pass through we forget
where we have been

LIBERTY

I love This

Every morning
somebody unlocks the statue
and lets in the day crew

first the welders who are fixing
the crack in the arm
that holds up the torch

and the elevator operators
the ticket sellers and the guides
and the next shift of police

the early ferries
land from the city
bringing visitors

born everywhere
to the cemented pedestal
under the huge toes

to follow signs
to the ticket booths
vendors conveniences

and to the guides to the crown and the arm
and the torch
whatever is safe

and the guides tell the names
of the sculptor and the donor
and explain why it is ours

also how much it weighs
and how many come to see it
in a year

and the name of the island
from which the foreigners
used to watch it

JOURNEY

Some time after the roofs fall in
the cars begin to come

on week ends the cars go to the country
this is the country

an old road has been found
crossing under a new one

the right clothes are put on
for visiting nobody who lives there

a broad footprint has been deciphered
crossing a cellar

in one of the empty houses
by the buried road

someone has driven a whole day
to declare how long it has been there

nobody knows anything
about who was here before

but nothing is real
until it can be sold

so a nice young couple
has cast in plaster

the broad foot
that went somewhere

the authentic white sole
rising from the white ground

so that people with cars
can take the foot home

to climb on their
blank walls

MEMORY

Climbing through a dark shower
I came to the edge of the mountain

I was a child
and everything was there

the flight of eagles the passage of warriors
watching the valley far below

the wind on the cliff the cold rain blowing upward
from the rock face

everything around me had burned
and I was coming back

walking on charcoal among the low green bushes
wet to the skin and wide awake

THE DUCK

The first time that I
was allowed to take out
the white canoe

because the lake was so still
in the evening
I slipped out on the long sky

of midsummer across the light
coming through the overturned
dark trees

I saw the duck catching
the colors of fire
as she moved over the bright glass

and I glided after
until she dove
and I followed with the white canoe

and look what I find
long afterwards
the world of the living

HEARING THE NAMES OF THE VALLEYS

Finally the old man is telling
the forgotten names
and the names of the stones they came from
for a long time I asked him the names
and when he says them at last
I hear no meaning
and cannot remember the sounds

I have lived without knowing
the names for the water
from one rock
and the water from another
and behind the names that I do not have
the color of water flows all day and all night
the old man tells me the name for it
and as he says it I forget it

there are names for the water
between here and there
between places now gone
except in the porcelain faces
on the tombstones
and places still here

and I ask him again
the name for the color of water
wanting to be able to say it
as though I had known it all my life
without giving it a thought

THE STRANGERS FROM THE HORIZON

Early one year
two ships came in to the foot of the mountain
from the sea in the first light of morning

we knew they were coming
though we had never seen them
they were black and bigger than houses

with teeth along the sides
and it is true
they had many arms

and cloaks filled with wind
clouds moving past us but they were not clouds
trees stopping before us but they were not trees

without having ever seen them we knew
without having ever seen us they knew
and we knew they knew each other

in another place they came from
and they knew that we knew
that they were not gods

they had a power for death that we wanted
and we went out to them taking things of ours
that they would surely need

CONQUEROR

When they start to wear your clothes
do their dreams become more like yours
who do they look like

when they start to use your language
do they say what you say
who are they in your words

when they start to use your money
do they need the same things you need
or do the things change

when they are converted to your gods
do you know who they are praying to
do you know who is praying

for you not to be there

NATIVE

Most afternoons
of this year which is written as a number
in my own hand
on the white plastic labels

I go down the slope
where mules I never saw
plowed in the sun and died
while I was in school

they were beaten to go
straight up the hill
so that in three years the rain
had washed all the topsoil

out past sea cliffs
and frigate birds
only a few years
after the forests were gone

now I go down past
a young mango tree
to the shelves made of wood
poisoned against decay

there under a roof
of palm fronds and chicken wire
I stare at the small native
plants in their plastic pots

here the 'ohia trees
filled with red flowers red birds
water notes flying music
the shining of the gods

here seeds from destroyed valleys
open late
beside their names in Latin
in the shade of leaves I have put there

PLACE

On the last day of the world
I would want to plant a tree

what for
not for the fruit

the tree that bears the fruit
is not the one that was planted

I want the tree that stands
in the earth for the first time

with the sun already
going down

and the water
touching its roots

in the earth full of the dead
and the clouds passing

one by one
over its leaves

WITNESS

I want to tell what the forests
were like

I will have to speak
in a forgotten language

CHORD

While Keats wrote they were cutting down the sandalwood forests
while he listened to the nightingale they heard their own axes
            echoing through the forests
while he sat in the walled garden on the hill outside the city they
            thought of their gardens dying far away on the mountain
while the sound of the words clawed at him they thought of their wives
while the tip of his pen travelled the iron they had coveted was
            hateful to them
while he thought of the Grecian woods they bled under red flowers
while he dreamed of wine the trees were falling from the trees
while he felt his heart they were hungry and their faith was sick
while the song broke over him they were in a secret place and they
            were cutting it forever
while he coughed they carried the trunks to the hole in the forest
            the size of a foreign ship
while he groaned on the voyage to Italy they fell on the trails and
            were broken
when he lay with the odes behind him the wood was sold for cannons
when he lay watching the window they came home and lay down
and an age arrived when everything was explained in another language

LOSING A LANGUAGE

A breath leaves the sentences and does not come back
yet the old still remember something that they could say

but they know now that such things are no longer believed
and the young have fewer words

many of the things the words were about
no longer exist

the noun for standing in mist by a haunted tree
the verb for I

the children will not repeat
the phrases their parents speak

somebody has persuaded them
that it is better to say everything differently

so that they can be admired somewhere
farther and farther away

where nothing that is here is known
we have little to say to each other

we are wrong and dark
in the eyes of the new owners

the radio is incomprehensible
the day is glass

when there is a voice at the door it is foreign
everywhere instead of a name there is a lie

nobody has seen it happening
nobody remembers

this is what the words were made
to prophesy

here are the extinct feathers
here is the rain we saw

THE LOST ORIGINALS

If only you had written our language
we would have remembered how you died

if you had wakened at our windows
we would have known who you were

we would have felt horror
at the pictures of you behind the barbed wire

from which you did not emerge
we would have returned to the shots of you lying dead with your kin

we would have ached to hear of your freezing
and your hunger in the hands of our own kind

we would have suffered at the degradation of your women
we would have studied you reverently

we would have repeated the words of your children
we would have been afraid for you

you would have made us ashamed and indignant
and righteous

we would have been proud of you
we would have mourned you

you would have survived
as we do

we might have believed
in a homeland

TERM

When all has been said
the road will be closed

when the old man has told
of walking as a child
on the road that the chief
built long ago

and has told of his father
walking with him
and his grandfather
when the road seemed to have been
there always along the sea
and has told of everyone he knew
and all his ancestors
coming that way
it will be closed

when the children have begged
to be able to go
to the sea there as they do
without having to be
rich or foreign
the road will be closed
for the rich and foreign
and the children will wait on them
where the road is now

where the thorny
kiawe trees smelling
of honey
dance in their shadows along the sand
the road will die
and turn into money at last
as the developers
themselves hope to do

what is sacred about a road anyway
what is sacred about any place
what is sacred about a language
what is sacred

what will we need to love
when it is all money
the rich will be rich
the foreign will be foreign
on the closed road

they are on their way already
their feet are the feet of ghosts
watching them is like watching a ship
leaving the shore
and seeing that it will never arrive

KANALOA

When he woke his mind was the west
and he could not remember waking

wherever he looked the sun was coming toward him
the moon was coming toward him

month after month the wind was coming toward him
behind the day the night was coming toward him

all the stars all the comets all the depth of the sea
all the darkness in the earth all the silence all the cold

all the heights were coming toward him
no one had been on the earth before him

all the stories were coming toward him
over the mountain

over the red water the black water
the moonlight

he had imagined the first mistake
all the humans are coming toward him with numbers

they are coming from the beginning to look for him
each of them finds him and he is different

they do not believe him at first
but he houses the ghosts of the trees

the ghosts of the animals
of the whales and the insects

he rises in dust he is burning he is smoke
behind him is nothing

he is the one who is already gone
he is fire flowing downward over the edge

he is the last he is the coming home
he might never have wakened

THE HORIZONS OF ROOMS

There have been rooms for such a short time
and now we think there is nothing else unless it is raining

or snowing or very late
with everyone else in another dark room

for a time beyond measure there were no rooms
and now many have forgotten the sky

the first room was made of stone and ice
and a fallen tree

with a heart beating in the room
and it was the ice that echoed it

because of a room a heart was born
in a room

and saw everything as a room
even what is called landscape

the present mountains were seen between moments
of remembering a room at another time

now there are more every year who remember childhood as a room
in which the person they were is thinking of a forest

but the first hands and first voices emerge in a room
with a ceiling

and later in another room
that ceiling appears again without the hands or voices

it is a room with an echoing wall
of ice

by now most sleeping is done in rooms
or on doorsteps leading to rooms

and the products of rooms
are carried on foot into the final uplands

we meet in a room
and go on from room to room

once there is a room
we know there was something before

and we go on living in the room as it has become
by good fortune

KNOCK

There is a knock on the door
and nobody is answering
a wave can be heard breaking

on a train from Florida
my mother offered me her bowl of peaches
when I was three
and did not want them
and I watched the white jacket
of the man carrying them away
on their tray along the corridor
while a silent grief rose in me

a plane roars into silence
they have to keep going
as though they were alive
they are hurtling toward the known world
which it is hopeless to reject
and death to accept

I open the door

THE BIOLOGY OF ART

Once at night
it begins
and you are the rest

whoever you are you see the first light
you see it arriving
like a star with you watching it

in the morning you can look at any tree
and see it has no age
and say so

after a long time you look down
into a valley without a name
after a long time as water you look up

THE ARCHAIC MAKER

The archaic maker is of course naive. If a man he listens. If a woman she listens. A child is listening. A train passes like an underground river. It enters a story.

The river cannot come back. The story goes on. It uses some form of representation. It does not really need much by way of gadgets, apart from words, singing, dancing, making pictures and objects that resemble living shapes. Things of its own devising.

The deafening river carries parents, children, entire families waking and sleeping homeward.

The story passes stone farms on green hillsides at the mouths of valleys running up into forests full of summer and unheard water.

In the story it is already tomorrow. A time of memories incorrect but powerful. Outside the window is the next of everything.

One of each.

But here is ancient today
itself
the air the living air
the still water

TRACING THE LETTERS

When I learn to read
I will know how green is spelled
when it is not green

already for all
the green of the years
there is only one word
even when the green is not there
and now the word is written down
and not only spoken

so it can be closed in the dark
against an unknown page
until another time

and still the green comes without a word
but when I see it
a word tells me it is green
and I believe it
even in the dark

I will be glad to learn to read
and be able to find
the stories with green in them
and to recognize
the green hands that were here before
the green eyelids and the eyes

THE ROSE BEETLE

It is said that you came from China
but you never saw China
you eat up the leaves here

your ancestors travelled blind in eggs
you arrive just after dark from underground
with a clicking whir in the first night
knowing by the smell what leaves to eat here
where you have wakened for the first time

the strawberry leaves foreign as you
the beans the orchid tree the eggplant
the old leaves of the heliconia the banana some palms
and the roses from everywhere but here
and the hibiscus from here the abutilons
the royal ilima

in the night you turn them into lace
into an arid net
into sky

like the sky long ago over China

A NOTE ABOUT THE AUTHOR

W. S. Merwin was born in New York City in 1927 and grew up in Union City, New Jersey, and in Scranton, Pennsylvania. From 1949 to 1951 he worked as a tutor in France, Portugal, and Majorca. After that, for several years he made the greater part of his living by translating from French, Spanish, Latin and Portuguese. Since 1954 several fellowships have been of great assistance. In addition to poetry, he has written articles, chiefly for *The Nation*, and radio scripts for the BBC. He has lived in Spain, England, France, Mexico and Hawaii, as well as New York City. His books of poetry are *A Mask for Janus* (1952), *The Dancing Bears* (1954), *Green with Beasts* (1956), *The Drunk in the Furnace* (1960), *The Moving Target* (1963), *The Lice* (1967), *The Carrier of Ladders* (1970) for which he was awarded the Pulitzer Prize, *Writings to an Unfinished Accompaniment* (1973), *The Compass Flower* (1977), *Opening the Hand* (1983) and *The Rain in the Trees* (1988). His translations include *The Poem of the Cid* (1959), *Spanish Ballads* (1960), *The Satires of Persius* (1961), *Lazarillo de Tormes* (1962), *The Song of Roland* (1963), *Selected Translations 1948–1968* (1968), for which he won the P.E.N. Translation Prize for 1968, *Transparence of the World*, a translation of his selection of poems by Jean Follain (1969), *Osip Mandelstam, Selected Poems* (with Clarence Brown) (1974) and *Selected Translations 1968–1978*. He has also published three books of prose, *The Miner's Pale Children* (1970), *Houses and Travellers* (1977) and *Unframed Originals* (1982). In 1974 he was awarded The Fellowship of the Academy of American Poets. In 1987 he received the Governor's Award for Literature of the state of Hawaii.

A NOTE ON THE TYPE

This book was set on the Linotype in Janson, a recutting made direct from type cast from matrices long thought to have been made by the Dutchman Anton Janson, who was a practicing type founder in Leipzig during the years 1668–1687. However, it has been conclusively demonstrated that these types are actually the work of Nicholas Kis (1650–1702), a Hungarian, who most probably learned his trade from the master Dutch type founder Dirk Voskens. The type is an excellent example of the influential and sturdy Dutch types that prevailed in England up to the time William Caslon (1692–1766) developed his own incomparable designs from them.

Composition by Heritage Printers, Inc.,
Charlotte, North Carolina
Printing and binding by Halliday Lithographers,
West Hanover, Massachusetts
Designed by Harry Ford